HOME STUDIES

HOME STUDIES

Prose Poems by Julie Gard

MANY VOICES PROJECT AWARD WINNER
#132

© 2015 by Julie Gard
First Edition
Library of Congress Control Number: 2014950578
ISBN: 978-0-89823-331-5
eISBN: 978-0-89823-341-4

Cover design by Rolf Busch
Interior design by Daniel Arthur Shudlick
Author photo by Jason Page

The publication of *Home Studies* is made possible by the generous support of Minnesota State University Moorhead, The McKnight Foundation, the Dawson Family Endowment, and other contributors to New Rivers Press.

For copyright permission, please contact Frederick T. Courtright at 570-839-7477 or permdude@eclipse.net

New Rivers Press is a nonprofit literary press associated with Minnesota State University Moorhead.

Alan Davis, Co-Director and Senior Editor
Suzzanne Kelley, Co-Director and Managing Editor
Kevin Carollo, MVP Poetry Coordinator
Vincent Reusch, MVP Prose Coordinator
Thom Tammaro, Poetry Editor
Nayt Rundquist, Assistant Production Editor
Wayne Gudmundson, Consultant

Publishing Interns:
Kjersti Maday, Kelly Mead, Mikaila Norman

Home Studies Book Team:
Val Anderson, Emily Jetvig, Kjersti Maday

Printed in the USA on acid free, archival-grade paper.

Home Studies is distributed nationally by Small Press Distribution

New Rivers Press
c/o MSUM
1104 7th Avenue South
Moorhead, MN 56563
www.newriverspress.com

For Michelle and Kristina

CONTENTS

Part III

*One is constantly wondering what sort of lives
other people lead, and how they take things.*

—George Eliot

I.

NEIGHBOR AS SELF
IN MANDAN, NORTH DAKOTA

It was all fun and games until their youngest was hit by a truck. We were the lesbian poet moms in the rambling blue farmhouse with the peace sign on one corner; they were the careful Christians in the classic yellow Victorian on the other. There was a mutual keeping of distance, a joint appreciation of the asphalt between us. Their daughter walked over each summer to invite ours to Vacation Bible School, which was thoughtful but annoying, as was the conversion van—get it?—that they parked in our favorite spot. I'm sure they had their issues too, like Lucinda Williams swearing from our windows, the way we'd let the weeds grow with the flowers, how our dog approached their dog in a not-so-Christlike manner. Then their son's skull cracked, and we stopped thinking about parking.

SIMPLE REPETITIONS

I do it and I watch it disappear. Every act is eaten by the next, by someone's. Every paper written is unwritten. Every grade given is forgotten. Every grade is a scar. Every house entered is unentered. Every parting is forgotten. Every parting a scar. Every dishcloth is dirty, then clean, then dirty. The child bangs her drum, learns her tune, and after the concert stuffs her music into the fire. My books grow lonely; they grow unread. They atrophy and unalphabetize. The snow collects under the shovel, bitterly scraping, scraping. The snow collects. The old man pushes at it, floats it, dividing white from white. The sky is a fractious mess of snow, a blur, a smear. The trees are coronary systems laid bare. They split a metaphor I did not write, one I wish I had.

ON SCARCITY

We are short a pair of brown shoes in our house. My partner put them on this morning and I'd already dressed in brown pants, striped socks, and a nice green shirt; all I needed were the shoes she was already wearing. I can't believe she took them off. I can't believe I asked her to. It's true they're mine, but I would cut out a kidney for her, even a lung, and so why not give her the shoes? They are perfectly wide and comfortable. She is older, smarter, and doesn't have as many nightmares. We should have better boundaries, at least different-sized feet. We should plan better. She says that it happens on Thursdays. There is something about the end of the week, when everything starts running out.

CONCEPTION

My child was conceived in Vladivostok while I read *The Idiot*, highlighting avidly, in a library six thousand miles away. She stole winter squash, eating it raw, while I cooked mine with raisins, butter, nutmeg, sea salt, olive oil, and wine. I missed her soft forehead all those years she scavenged acorns while I was in graduate school; all those years she hid where she could while I studied fiction.

PROCESSIONS

I dreamt of my grandfather crossing the road, mute but his silence was kind. He was the one I didn't know past nine. He is frozen in junior fiction. He is sweating in the sun on the road. He is touching corn he never even saw. His shop is dusty; it is still there. The ledgers and the lumberyard, a few boards drying at dusk. Things long to be used again, like his fingers forming numbers, balancing columns, saving for a trip back to the war zone. His cancer was an orange in that belly we leaned on while he read. There was nothing to know then. All that existed was what I could touch. Pain led to pleasure: a broken leg to a week of TV, sunburn to a bowl of strawberries. His funeral to the dinner afterwards: fizz-pink Shirley Temples, one after another at the bar.

HOME FRONT

Two men came out to clean the vents, and the old woman next door saw the truck and big hose. She waved them over with her cane. She told them we were sinners from Minneapolis.

The vent cleaners came back and one said, We can't do her vents. We don't do vents that old. I gave her another number. I don't like when people talk. I said to him, She's old. She's just holding on.

And it's true. I am glad when her pocked Chevy's gone for an hour on Sundays, since it means she's still alive. She puts out her garbage too late every Tuesday, and it sits there all week in the snow. Sometimes fragments blow into our yard, like the picture of squinting men eating camp breakfast in Medora, 1948. They look so hungry.

Tacit Agreements

She likes to have a bit of things left, a scrap, a swig, a crumb. I tend to finish it all, clear the shelf, eat the last, but I don't anymore — when I remember. Now I leave an eighth of red pepper to wilt in the crisper, a wrapped handful of cabbage. I do not take the final sliver of good cheese. Or I do, but I know that I am taking it from her.

COMMUNION

Depression is so boring. Your whole life goes by and all you've done is hold on. You've grabbed onto broomsticks, mop handles, job titles and children, limbs of lovers and their thick, smooth hair. They keep you afloat until the next season when the day might come that you enjoy a spot of t'ai chi or an evening walk on a shell-ground beach. The poke of the shells on your feet makes the sunset quicken. You realize your luck at the family who found you one Saturday night in the glow of a Disney special, for here you all are together under one potentially lethal electric blanket. You bite your lip with fierce love, and depression is no match. You have triumphed until the next morning, when you consider not getting up but always get up, like your father. Is this what happened? The struggling sadness, the unmade beauty. I mean the unmade bed. But you make it, you do, twice for good measure.

DOUBLE REST

In a world of quiet, there is always more room for quiet. It comes after something terrible or fantastic. Quiet descends before annihilation or a miracle. In the quietest part of a person is the time before sound took shape. As I started to come into being, when did I first hear? When did the roaring of my mother's blood begin, not just in my cells but in my ears? I can hear it when she visits, and after she goes.

FRACTALS

Don't touch me, my daughter says half the time I reach out. The other half she takes my hand, leans into me. The other half of the time, she's the one reaching for me. When she says don't touch me, half of the time she's already sitting next to me with her left side pressed against my right. Half of the time, she is across the room and I'm reading a book. She wants to know if it's a book about her. Then she's angry, if it is or if it's not.

MUSE

All I know is that her name is Hildegard. She is seventy and shovels with regularity. At sunrise her track blinds open; at dusk they close. I cannot see beyond them. There is never a spot of trash in the yard. I would give a pint of blood for a change of view, to look out on a crooked street in Oslo. The open prairie would be unmooring, but I'd prefer it aesthetically. Old boardwalk and dune and gravelly sea, even broken blue sign of a laundromat. But the little green house of an old woman is the view from my writing desk. Its cockeyed tin chimney breathes smoke that spells, *you won't live here forever.*

My Parents Talk about Moving

Your father was alone with the three of you during the week, my mother says. I stayed with Mom and Pop to finish graduate school. My father nods. I brought you to church alone, he says, one and three and five. Laur tried to climb the ladder while I painted the house. Remember how we covered the upstairs in one day with that rented spray painter? my mother asks. There just wasn't time for the roller. The neighbors were friendly, she says, but we have never gotten close.

CARNAL STRUGGLE, 2006

There's no way to win in bed, in dreams. You can only lie beside me making love to a U.S. president who repulses you, while I pluck goose poop from a nylon car seat. In reality, your foot is sweet against mine. The dog between us scratches all night, making wounds where there were none. This indelible life.

ON HONOR

Some people know their duty and do it: release the bomb, fix the sentence. You should see them with their coffee in the morning, the way their legs drop out of the car. The bus driver whistles Purcell's "Faerie Queen" and wears her sunglasses over bifocals at the same slant every day. My uncle carries bodies out of nursing homes and is always respectful and quiet. He smoothes down his white hand-kerchief and follows traffic laws. I am the writing professor who dreams of inspiring her students, and I try out for the same part every day. Maybe tomorrow I will get it.

ALMOST, NOT QUITE, SOMEWHERE

Fifteen years ago, sprawled on the kitchen floor of a summer apartment, two weeks before the refrigerator went out and the room filled with the stench of rotting food, I played guitar for three hours, the three chords I knew. I sang about the house I would live in someday, the house I live in now. I sang about staying for thirty years, though tomorrow we are moving. One winter break, I pecked at the piano every day for a week, trying to make a four-part arrangement of a Joni Mitchell song. It never came to anything—the red wine, the wind blowing out of Africa, my frustration with finding the proper time signature. Flying over the Atlantic soon after graduation, I scribbled a note that went through the wash. It contained a part of myself that's the only real part. I am constantly losing it. It is all that remains.

ALIGNMENT'S WIT

After seven years together, my partner and I finally write the same poem. The odds were quite good, actually, as she approached prose poetry from verse and I from story, that we'd meet in the middle with a short strip of words about our daughter. Statistically it's bound to happen, that two lovers sharing a bed would write the same sentence, that two inventors standing on opposite ends of earth's longest sidewalk would create the same amalgam at the same time. Who gets the patent then, the riches, the byline, the fame? We don't wish to share. We do not collaborate. So we trade our sheets of paper, read them, trade them back. After seven more years we will tire of this, but I love the way that she says, that I say, she is tumbleweed in the morning.

YOU CAN ALWAYS DO IT AGAIN

Every day I clean the kitchen. Never too clean, just clean enough. The counters we touch are white to the eye and the dishwasher almost works on "pot scrub." Its sound is the sound of working. I make dinner. Sometimes it is fresh. I chop the freshness. Rutabagas, pizza, apples and expensive cheese, mac and cheap cheese. Wholesome and unwholesome. I soak the burners in vinegar and scrub them. I replace them. A pot of rice boils over and one burner smokes. I clean it again, only this time not as clean, but at least it doesn't smoke. I mop the floor just twice a year at Thanksgiving and Easter. I never dust, just brush at cobwebs that grow too obvious. Seed pods stick in the window screen. The backyard fills with dog droppings. Snow collects, acidic and pure. I make lists and lose them, write poems and lose them. Tell me where you found this one.

II.

In the summer of 2006, a neighbor tried to burn our house down. These objects are from the thrift shop where he worked.

Silver Bracelet, $1.00

A simple form is best for first. There is something to say of eternity here, one life in one forged curve. One can take sides in a physical world where a metal ring forms in and out. One cannot take sides where the inner eye sees a rounded line and the lamp sees silver. Each meaning molten to the next in the metal itself, each meaning forged by heat.

American Flag, 10¢

I moved to North Dakota. I'm supposed to write about space. I'm supposed to be opened and stunned by sky and feel free and write about it. I'm not supposed to say how my mind grows fences. They go up in my poems, in my brain, in the town. Someone lonely plants them in cold edges of soil. This person works hard all day.

SMILING SQUIRREL PIN, 40¢

He started by raking the leaves. Then in winter he shoveled the walk, scraping, scraping. He played with the neighborhood children, gave us mints and other objects. He sent twenty pages of handwritten Bible verse, ending with *I want to be her daddy.* We told him our daughter had parents. Next the porch was heaped with lingerie. I talked with his landlady, not the police. You have to spread the word but not by bothering folks, she said. Months passed.

SILVER CHEESE KNIFE, 20¢

A fine, flowered knife for spreading soft cheese, the orange
kind with almonds my father likes. This knife has other
uses, like slicing banana or cutting through cranberry roll.
The use of a knife depends upon the family.

Faux Stained Glass Jesus, PRICE UNMARKED

The lamb and her flag, bleeding ribbon in wind, ten flowers with crimson centers. The son of God points south to where the air is said to be warm. One teardrop rests between his eyes like the mark on a Hindu wife. His halo puffs a trail of dust. His frame is thick plastic painted like wood, his image thin plastic painted like glass. The Lord is not angry, just worried. You should, he thinks, but I'm not sure you will. And the caged lamb smiles for some reason.

BICYCLE PLAYING CARDS, 60¢

He watched me paint the fence, so I went inside. We drove thousands of miles to the ocean. While we swam, he set the fire. We came home and found the attempt. We came home and everything was fine, except for the fact that he'd tried. The detective came, and I gave him the letters and objects. Our neighbor confessed he had wanted to make our walls black. *One lady in that house, can't remember her name, told me not to talk to the other.* This made him angry, though it never even happened.

WHITE DOILY, 20¢

In every life is a scrap of beauty, man or mechanically made. In every life there is justice, encompassing the arc of the life or pushed to the far corner of the piano. We went next door to tell his landlady her tenant was in jail. She told us he kept stuffed animals like a child would. She invited us down to see his basement room, but we declined, given the upcoming trial. I'll give that boy a talking to when he comes home, she said. You don't go setting fire to people's houses. My partner said, He isn't coming home.

J.C. PENNEY BUTTON COVERS, 40¢

There's a button for every time I said no. Because of these small round refusals, he took a match to our house. Now three blocks over, he sits in jail. I drive through quiet rain. You should see the brush along the highway now. Five days into frost, it is fire.

Deep Sea Jelly Candle, 30¢

Main Street, under construction, is suddenly underwater in an early-morning dream. Waves drench signs for the fall election. The mayor almost died from heart failure last year, his daughter from cancer this summer. Now they coach sixth-grade girls' basketball. I love to watch them breathe. The rumor flies he is out on bail, but I walk to the store anyway. My partner keeps fixing the porch. Our daughter plays in her Halloween wig and everything moves a bit slow. I return home with canned sauerkraut and call the county jail. It is not true. See how we go on.

Tetra Terrafauna Vitaminized Hermit Crab Meal, 60¢

Our neighbor pleads guilty at the pretrial hearing. There will be no extension of what is seen as our shame. I do not shake until I teach the next day, and then I do, in front of my class. I stretch so far into what I am not that words for the starving repeat in my head: apple, ethoxyquin, feather meal.

Wooden Smokey the Bear Ruler, 10¢

There is something about a birch ruler rubbed by November finger. Squash in the oven with wine-baked chicken, the house almost clean, air almost pure. Life is almost even and contentment almost measurable. My child is almost happy and my partner almost well. I renew our home insurance policy. We are close to the line either way.

CROSS OF JOY, 50¢

This cross tells me what I can bear, anything. It's a breakable solid inscribed with a mandate: Joy. The church folk call redemption what is loneliness stitched with anger. Aesthetically the cross speaks to me, but I refuse its message. Let us join together in our lack of understanding, our communion this common air. You breathe what has gone through my body. In response, I take you in.

Silver Teaspoon, 40¢

The arsonist's absence in small things: snow coating the walk, our standing house. Two phone books delivered to the porch next door, one marked owner and one marked tenant.

CLIFF'S NOTES FOR DICKENS'
HARD TIMES, 20¢

Life here is easy, a ruler-straight layer of cloud behind western trees. In a ship I would sail through branches, torn barnacle in hand. This December is so mellow that it seems the world will end. Three blocks away they bring him meals, just like his landlady would do. The food isn't bad and it's free and they bring it. He never had a choice. This is one theory.

Wooden Earrings, 50¢

I shovel his landlady's walk. He is no longer here to do it. I think, if I write of this later, I am making a poem by shoveling. I am writing without writing; I am pushing at meaning. I am writing with this shovel, telling in snow.

CAGED BEAR FROM GLACIER PARK, 50¢

From Ruben Bentz to John Harell in Linten, Texas: As a Gift. Four walls at the county jail, feet in heavy glue. Everyone pays attention when he burns, and otherwise no one but the minister. The addicted mother, the absent father, brain damage from the start. *I had a sister too, but Ma dropped her down the steps.* She falls into the gift's red mouth.

FOUR STEM BUMPERS, ¾", 10¢

Our neighbor shelved this object in 1997, and no one has touched it since. He didn't think of it later himself, nor did the woman up front who counts purchases slowly and wrinkles them into bags. The package is smeared with its price in green crayon. It would never be bought so I bought it, to the sound of the passing train.

Blue Glass Candleholder, 50¢

Confront and avoid the older brother who murdered. The blue dress of the old woman was limp, marked with water and blood. Our neighbor longs for communion and pork rinds, for the word that almost saves.

Empty Frame with Symmetrical Flowers, 20¢

When I was young, I had plenty to say. I became mute
when older, held in by the curve of my own chest cage.
Seeing end before beginning: awful use for imagination.
This frame holds what I choose, half the white laundry
basket and floorboards in sun. Alarm clock, chest and
magazine rack. Windowpane, driveway, mud puddle.
The minister piles our neighbor's things in the back of a
tan pickup. The truck pulls out of the frame.

Genuine Ace Hard Rubber Comb, 20¢

I can play this comb like an instrument, one that hums whenever I breathe. The words to the song are, Where will we go? How will we get there? In his basement room, he kept a picture of his mother. His landlady brings us dented cans of green beans and tells us she looked normal, like a real nice woman. In a crazy season, stuck in a numb dark year, one can usually force a smile.

PINK BATH SOAP, ½ BAR, 10¢

In Fargo, 1978, his mother was evicted and he burned the landlord's house down. There were three other arsons as well. His confessions are pieces of paper I have never seen, never touched. Yet because of the crime, we are unclean.

MOOD RING, 25¢

Tilted sideways, the clear stone is red. Sociological theories of violence make each victimizer victim. Fifty-four years and two moods: saved and angry. The courtroom holds the minister, judge, lawyers, landlady, stenographer, press, and us. Our neighbor's hair is knotted. His voice rusts as he speaks. The wooden bench becomes my back as the prosecutor reads our daughter's words: The fire was a nightmare. In blaze orange, he gets eight years.

TOUCHED BY THE FIRE: LUKE/ACTS IN THE TODAY'S ENGLISH VERSION, 60¢

My father read books like this once, back when he fumbled through winter days of teaching in dark glasses. Ohio transplant in Philadelphia soil, spaghetti dinners for Methodist young adults, my mother across town in her nursing school cloisters. They searched in similar pages. The Vietnam War burned in passages. They were only starting out. Almost forty years later, I do not read the book that brought them together, but I know such miracles do occur. Heat can crack the seed.

DOLL HANDS, ONE PAIR, 10¢

These hands full of air cannot sign what they've seen. They have witnessed blunt crimes and deep errors. Every unmade doll and misinterpreted gesture, every plastic souvenir from every accidental war. They tell me it could happen anywhere. They assure me he'll never come back. But we're going, my own hands sign. I form leaving with my fingers.

GOODY FOAM ROLLERS, 10 LARGE, 50¢

We decide the house put out the fire, good spirits from 1896. I can sit on the porch again this spring as the elm buds green and thicken. Last year I gave him an Easter basket; we were grateful for his work in the yard. How stupid that now appears. He is gone and no one watches me plan a life in another town. As he wished, we will not forget him. The mind does not close without opening. Neither does the world.

III.

WHITE APPROACH

A patch of birch bark is the surface of a lake, its lenticels silver fish, siscowet, paperbelly, moving just beneath the surface, that or elegant canoes. I did not grow up among birches and learned late the gravity and weightlessness of winter, moving on skis between tree ghosts threading lit pink sky. At summer solstice, their blur of tremoring leaves is translucent green music, the forest's life and afterlife.

Behind glass in Novgorod, words etched into birch bark eight hundred years ago preserve harvests, trades, and love. White trees called me north into as much wisdom as I could bear, closer to the heart I lost, the heart I look for.

A Boy Is Sent Back to Russia

A boy is sent back to Russia with a pack of crayons, a lollipop, and a pinned-on note. Life together in the squat blue house in Tennessee, which he said he'd burn down with the people in it, was not working for his new mother. Personally, we were prepared for fire or shit smeared on the walls. Better to be ready for too much.

Math homework was a challenge for this family, says the article in the paper. How many disrupted adoptions, I wonder, can be traced back to word problems? We lost a kitchen table to them, and a pane of glass in a French door. We did not, however, lose our daughter, not even to geometry, not even to loss.

AUBADE

To the dog who chases the sheet in circles, to the squirrel who walks a frosted highwire, to the bundled old couple whose sneakers move in white unison, to the teenager with a raw throat. To the succession of cats inspecting my desk, to the garbage can at the lip of the road, to the peak of the porch and dendrite hope of the lilac, to the growl of engine and the warmth of vanilla tea. To the creak of my partner's footsteps, to the zen intonations of Cathy Werzer, to the public radio pledge drive, to the eight hundred in Chile, to the twelve thousand in Haiti. To my students, willing them the foresight to make it to class today. To the ones who will not make it.

CHILD'S BLOCK PUZZLE

Cabbage is a green world. Tomato is shaded and subtle, mysterious spots and reaching stem. Cucumber is a bursting rocket, whimsical and prickled, taking off into white night, and the infinite, important Russian beet swells jauntily. Peapod, slender and mysterious, slants away from answer toward question.

A teething child would bite each block, like my daughter if she'd had toys. She would have tasted glue and paper, felt dense wood in her wet fist. She paints them black now, but long before I met her, she had the tiny, translucent nails of every child in every country, the unmarked fingers. What they held became her.

Rush Hour

That is my own Geo Metro going by, my own self driving past me making slush sounds on the road, the driver putting on lip balm and balancing a jar of tea. My God, she looks like me. Smoothing and puffing red hair, mind on fourteen things at once, clearly bored and overwhelmed. 'Tis a special talent, to be a thrill-seeking creature of habit. I watch her remember an unsigned permission slip, abandoned novella, sore on the dog's belly, and swerve but stay on the road, pouring tea onto the floor mat. The determined little engine rumbles. Such good mileage in that car, such derring-do.

ART OF PERSUASION

I understand that your mother was murdered, but you must keep coming to class. This is what she would want, her last thought before being dumped on the snow bank, for her daughter to prove the knife wrong. Don't start something and not finish, like the student who disappeared after *her* mother won ten thousand in the state lottery. I know it's material, the cash, the body, but the life of the mind is eternal.

Do it because you moved across the state line for school, remade all your plans, and I promise to add commas and take them away just like I used to. The computers will glow all around us, and you'll learn that words, if nothing else, make sense.

TEMPORARY CAREER-SWITCH
DAYDREAM

I want to work in an empty room with a desk beneath one window. I want a job with a stack of ledgers, entirely copying numbers. Neat rows straight as teeth, like my grandfather made in his lumber company records. There was sawdust in his office and it's drifting into mine. The window glows pale yellow and I can't see through the glass. I earn enough for food, enough to raise my daughter, but not a penny more. I don't write a number more. When I put down the pen and cross the room, the ledgers stay closed on the desk. They do not follow me out the door. Everything is wooden, including the door. There are no people. Unless I speak, there is no voice.

SWIMMING

My partner's right eye was red and sore yesterday, so last night in my dream, my deceased grandmother's right nipple was inflamed, bumpy and red, while her left one hardly existed. That's how they've been, she said to a dear old friend as they changed at the YWCA. Meanwhile, the patch of dry skin to the right of my nose had swelled into a cluster of hard, unpoppable cysts, one of which turned purple and angry. I was told by a dog in a white lab coat, this is not the good kind, and his fatalism was infectious.

FOR A SECOND NO HAND

My girl saw me waving at the window, so she waved back
from the car. From the second floor I watched one small
hand unfold, the other around the ceramic mug I poured
her coffee into this morning. For a second no hand on
the wheel, the Subaru suspended at an angle in the street.
Our eyes met through layers of glass. That's how I found
her, through all of these chances.

VISITATION

I eat dinner with my mother and father. It is rarely just the three of us anymore, and I imagine we are all who are left. We link our hands to pray and the circle is small. The dining room table stretches out and we take up just one end. Something has happened to everyone we love, and now we are nothing but memory. This must be what happens in war. A family is destroyed, just a few members strangely remaining. Each survivor carries four, five spirits. They eat dinner on this side; they eat on the other.

TICKS

In the North Woods in June, you learn to write with ticks crawling up your legs. You go on with conversation, pick them off in the middle of sentences, hold them tightly between thumb and forefinger, up to four at a time. You check the dog and mistake his vestigial nipple for a tick. There is one close to his privates and you pluck it gently, crooning. You've never found one on you full, only searching, ascending, seeking the perfect plot of skin. They take so long to dig in, you wonder how they make a living. You burn them with matches which you'd do to no other creature, only this one. They have never harmed you, but you prosecute based on intent. Perhaps they only crave a little warmth, but you see them, oiled and impossibly flat, and you assume you know. You assure the dog that you know.

LARGE BRASS KEY

The purpose of life is creation; the purpose is my daughter. At any moment, one can interrupt the other. She bursts into the room while I'm writing; my mind drifts to a poem in the middle of her sentence. My daughter is real in the kitchen — I can hear her making a sandwich — but this page is real in my study, like the key she found on a side street off Nevsky. I told her it opened Russia. Mom, stop, she said, but she brought it home. Now we share this one thing comfortably, the key that's in her room and in my mind.

ORDINARY PEOPLE

A friend turns fifty today, and I recall meeting her son. He sat in their public housing apartment, bare except for her wall-sized collages, reading a book on how to be a pimp. That was ten years ago. These days he flies all over the country and she's not sure why. She doesn't ask. He gets up early and drives in the dark to the airport. He wears a nice shirt and checks his watch. He is a business traveler with newspaper hiding his knees. From his seat in coach he sees ravaged sunrise, like the one last flight but different. Always through the window, on the other side of something.

NOTE TO SELF

I fell down the stairs this morning, twisting my arm and drowning myself in tea. Varnished wood met muscle and bone, phone and cup and notebook flew. A state of shock — time to stir the chili — and then why me? followed by acceptance: clean up the mess, take off tea-stained robe and godforsaken slippers. I stirred chili in my underwear this morning with a bag of frozen peas stuck down them. I would complain to the authorities, but they sleep and steer clear of the winter streets. I am on my own.

HOMAGE TO LYDIA DAVIS

A was done with B's rudeness, and because B would not write an apology note to A, C refused to help blow-dry B's hair. The problem this time was B's shirt, which A felt was too low-cut when B leaned over. As C in this situation I agreed, yet based on observation of area teens, found the neckline within current standards of decency. Of course, as one of two mothers bracketing B, I would have preferred that the neckline be higher. As C, I would certainly not have allowed it to go any lower. And so A was tired of the rudeness, the meanness, and C was ashamed that it still went on, while B was simply unhappy with wet hair, eating granola bars for breakfast and reading the funnies. In other news, a power plant in Connecticut exploded while workers were clearing the gas lines and the whole thing plumed like a hibachi grill. Five men died — let's call them D through H — replacing A, B, and C altogether in this story.

MAKE YOUR OWN FUN

My love and I celebrated Valentine's Day by bird-calling in an echoing underpass, counting origami peace cranes in snowy pines, using the men's restroom at the co-op, rearranging furniture at Starbucks, winking at a child in a star-covered snowsuit, and joy-riding through Superior, Wisconsin past collapsing turreted beauties, a life-sized plastic Packers doll on a shiny green porch, a second-floor door opening into nowhere, intricate matchsticks of handicapped accessible ramps, and brownstones smattered with sheets of tin. We parked at Red Lobster but crossed the street for Thai, sucked down coconut milk, cruised to Wrenshall, lit a hundred-year-old woodstove, peed in the snow, crawled into a cold bed, crawled out of a warm bed when the cabin owners arrived, into bed, out of bed, no room at the motel, and performed psycho-analysis on ourselves and others.

POEM TO LIVE BY

I have no idea how to live. Our daughter ran away, the days grew shorter, your father died. The car would not stop and I slid on steep ice, almost into the lake. All winter I tried to exist without thought, like a blank sheet of paper. To be empty of expectation and fear, to freeze into one pattern. But a fire burned in my gut; I could see it through my skin.

She did come back, and I swerved the car into an abandoned lot just in time. Your father became the woods where he fell, having shown us how to die. Our daughter listens for him from our place in the circle, in the snow-pressed arc of the stopping wheels of the car.

ACKNOWLEDGEMENTS

This book is the culmination of a decade of writing and living, and I am grateful to many for their influence, inspiration and advice. My deepest thanks go out to all the good neighbors in Pennsylvania, New Jersey, Iowa, North Dakota, Russia, and Minnesota; supportive, inspiring colleagues and students at the University of Wisconsin Superior, Wisconsin Indianhead Technical College, and Bismarck State College; wise mentors Valerie Miner and Julie Schumacher; the women of Moon Group and Sing! A Women's Chorus; and Susan Taylor, Wayne Smith, Maureen Aitken, and the writing group pups. Gratitude to Jayson Iwen, for the perfect title; Amy Groshek, for helpful feedback at just the right time; Jamie White-Farnham, for the imaginary office pass-through; Vineet Shende, for music from fire; and Sheila Packa and Kathy McTavish, for friendship and art in life. Deep appreciation to Paul and Claudia Gard, Peter Gard, Lauren Gard, and our beautiful extended family, for origins and ongoing support; to my grandparents, for love from the ancestor world; and to Annie and Steve Luttinen, AnnMarie Kajencki, Janelle Masters, Colleen Thomas, Melissa Kreider, the Ferronis, the Kukuyans, the Matthees, the Petersons, the Wengers, and the Miklasevics family, for endless wit and sustenance. Thank you to Raymone Kral and Lisa Hay, for getting it; Sheila Whalen, for believing in the early stories; the Arrowhead Regional Arts Council, for vital support; Suzzanne Kelley, Emily Jetvis, Kjersti Maday, Val Anderson, and Nayt Rundquist of New Rivers Press, for thoughtful and thorough editing and guidance; and Ditcher, George, Jenna, and KitKat, for never fearing to tread on a manuscript. Deepest gratitude to my partner, the poet Michelle Matthees, for fifteen years and counting of intertwined and independent writing and life, and to my daughter, Kristina Alekseevna, for being the bravest and most stylish person I know.

CREDITS

Grateful acknowledgement is made to the editors and staff members of the following publications in which these poems first appeared:

In Posse Review: "Ordinary People"
The Light Ekphrastic: "Make Your Own Fun"
Literary Mama: "Homage to Lydia Davis" (as "Word Problem") and "Conception"
New Purlieu Review: "Fractals"
Prick of the Spindle: "Procession" and "Communion"
The Prose-Poem Project: "Simple Repetitions" and "You Can Always Do It Again"
Tiger's Eye Journal: "Temporary Career Switch Daydream"
Tiger's Eye Press: "Large Brass Key" and "Child's Block Puzzle" in chapbook *Russia in 17 Objects*
Two Hawks Quarterly: "Art of Persuasion"
What Doesn't Kill You. . . Press 53, Winston-Salem, NC: Part II as "Thin Bits of Evidence"
When We Become Weavers: Queer Female Poets on the Midwestern Experience. Squares and Rebels Press, Minneapolis: "Neighbor as Self in Mandan, North Dakota," "On Scarcity," "Carnal Struggle, 2006," and "Ticks"

Selected poems were featured on radio programs *The Beat* (KAXE) and *Women's World* (KUMD). Selected poems from Part II of *Home Studies* were set to music for voice and string quartet by composer Vineet Shende. The resulting song cycle, *Thin Bits of Evidence,* debuted at Bowdoin College, Brunswick, ME on April 9, 2014. Selected poems from Part II were also featured in the Minnesota State Art Board's 2009 Art of Recovery Exhibit.

Epigraph: George Eliot. *Middlemarch.* Boston: Houghton Mifflin, 1968 (238).

"White Approach" was inspired by the photograph "Blue Stream" by Heidi Mae Niska.

ABOUT THE AUTHOR

Julie Gard received her BA in English from Grinnell College and her MFA in Creative Writing from the University of Minnesota. Publications include *Russia in 17 Objects,* which was awarded first place in the Tiger's Eye Press Chapbook Contest in 2010, and *Obscura: The Daguerreotype Series,* released by Finishing Line Press in 2007. Her poetry collection *Home Studies* was the 2013 recipient of the Many Voices Project Prize from New Rivers Press. She is the recipient of grants from the Fulbright Foundation, the Barbara Deming Memorial Fund, and the Arrowhead Regional Arts Council. Gard is Associate Professor of Writing at the University of Wisconsin Superior and lives with her partner, the poet Michelle Matthees, in Duluth, Minnesota.

ABOUT NEW RIVERS PRESS

New Rivers Press emerged from a drafty Massachusetts barn in winter 1968. Intent on publishing work by new and emerging poets, founder C. W. "Bill" Truesdale labored for weeks over an old Chandler & Price letterpress to publish three hundred fifty copies of Margaret Randall's collection, *So Many Rooms Has a House But One Roof.*

Nearly four hundred titles later, New Rivers, a nonprofit and now teaching press based since 2001 at Minnesota State University Moorhead, has remained true to Bill's goal of publishing the best new literature—poetry and prose—from new, emerging, and established writers.

New Rivers Press authors range in age from twenty to eighty-nine. They include a silversmith, a carpenter, a geneticist, a monk, a tree-trimmer, and a rock musician. They hail from cities such as Christchurch, Honolulu, New Orleans, New York City, Northfield (Minnesota), and Prague.

Charles Baxter, one of the first authors with New Rivers, calls the press "the hidden backbone of the American literary tradition." Continuing this tradition, in 1981 New Rivers began to sponsor the Minnesota Voices Project (now called Many Voices Project) competition. It is one of the oldest literary competitions in the United States, bringing recognition and attention to emerging writers. Other New Rivers publications include the American Fiction Series, the American Poetry Series, New Rivers Abroad, and the Electronic Book Series.

Please visit our website newriverspress.com for more information.

Many Voices Project
Award Winners

("OP" indicates that the paper copy is out of print; "e-book" indicates that the title is available as an electronic publication.)

#35 *Burning the Prairie*, John Reinhard
#34 *Last Summer*, Davida Kilgore (OP)
#33 *The High Price of Everything*, Kathleen Coskran
#32 *Storm Lines*, Warren Woessner (OP)
#31 *Dying Old and Dying Young*, Susan Williams
#30 *Once, A Lotus Garden*, Jessica Saiki (OP)
#28 *The Wind*, Patricia Barone
#27 *All Manner of Monks*, Benet Tvedten (OP)
#26 *Flash Paper*, Theresa Pappas (OP)
#25 *Tap Dancing for Big Mom*, Roseann Lloyd
#24 *Twelve Below Zero*, Anthony Bukoski (OP)
#23 *Locomotion*, Elizabeth Evans (OP)
#22 *What I Cannot Say, I Will Say*, Monica Ochtrup
#21 *Descent of Heaven Over the Lake*, Sheryl Noethe (OP)
#20 *Matty's Heart*, C.J. Hribal (OP)
#19 *Stars Above, Stars Below*, Margaret Hasse (OP)
#18 *Golf Ball Diver*, Neal Bowers (OP)
#17 *The Weird Kid*, Mark Vinz (OP)
#16 *Morning Windows*, Michael Moos (OP)
#15 *Powers*, Marisha Chamberlain (OP)
#14 *Suspicious Origins*, Perry Glasser (OP)
#13 *Blenheim Palace*, Wendy Parrish (OP)
#12 *Rivers, Stories, Houses, Dreams*,
    Madelon Sprengnether
#11 *We'll Come When It Rains*, Yvette Nelson (OP)
#10 *Different Arrangements*, Sharon Chmielarz
#9 *Casualties*, Katherine Carlson
#8 *Night Sale*, Richard Broderick
#7 *When I Was a Father*, Alvaro Carona-Hine (OP)
#6 *Changing the Past*, Laurie Taylor (OP)
#5 *I Live in the Watchmaker's Town*, Ruth Roston (OP)
#4 *Normal Heart*, Madelon Gohlke (OP)
#3 *Heron Dancer*, John Solensten
#2 *The Reconstruction of Light*, John Minczeski (OP)
#1 *Household Wounds*, Deborah Keenan (OP)